Sea of Destiny

Sea of Destiny

Amber Nightingale

Sea of Destiny
Copyright © 2020 Amber Nightingale
All rights reserved.
First edition: November 2020

Disclosure: The information in this book is not a substitute for medical care and Amber Nightingale is not liable for anything whatsoever. Reader accepts full responsibility.

ISBN- 978-1-71687-163-4

Imprint: Lulu.com

Also by Amber Nightingale

Brave Soul: A healer's journey into spiritual awakening

Reiki Healing For The Modern World: A guide for teachers and students alike

ACKNOWLEDGMENTS

I would like to thank my family, who are my biggest supporters.

I dedicate this book to my baby princess.
I love you.

CONTENTS

"If our view of heaven is a passing cloud in this lifetime, Amber's words are a gentle rain- always refreshing, always renewing and always restoring the beauty of a spiritual life." – Sean J.

CHAPTER 1

The Skyline of Manhattan

I stepped off the platform and into the unknown. It was December, as the cold air tugged at my scarf around my neck. I had been waiting for this moment for seven years, ever since I had the premonition that I would end up in NYC as part of my path and calling. I made up my mind to go it alone. I wanted to challenge myself and see if I could venture to NYC and navigate a place I had never been.

The ferry tugged forth, as I saw the cityscape before me, as wide as the eye could see. I looked east and west, as it spanned for miles, a never-ending sea scape of skyscrapers, buses, taxis and cars. I was here. The closer the ferry got to the entrance of NYC, the greater the anticipation and my heart danced with excitement. I departed from the ferry with high expectations that with my map and GPS, that I would be able to navigate the streets of one of the biggest cities in the world.

My expectations were matched

as I navigated the streets with ease. I grabbed a taxi to take me to the bookstore on 14th street in Manhattan for my book signing. I got out half-way there as traffic was at a standstill and started walking as fast as I could almost in a sprint to make it to the bookstore on time.

I passed Broadway Street walking briskly for another 15 minutes or so, made a hard left and entered the bookstore with 15 minutes to spare. My books were displayed in the front as the employees greeted me warmly. They had a chair for me in the back with others next to it for readers to sit at. Then the magic happened. Customers arrived and sat down in front of me, intrigued at what I had to say. I felt in my element. My soul was at peace and fulfilled as I had waited for this moment for so long.

I explained who I was, why I was there, what I could offer and how I could help others through my work. I knew in my heart that I was meant to be there.

My old life had departed and my soul was in the present. The readers and I had beautiful conversations between us. I could see it in their eyes as they listened to my words that I was in the place I was meant to be. I considered NYC my home. As I left the bookstore and waved for a taxi out front, my soul was completely filled with reverence and harmony.

The cab driver's name was Rick. He had a kind demeanor about him as he talked about his travels around NYC. He knew every road, alley and street and got me to Rockefeller Center faster than anyone I had ever seen. He screeched to a halt at my destination and I thanked him for his quick service and gave him a big tip. I wanted to see the Christmas tree as it was only two weeks before Christmas. The hustle and bustle of people everywhere was almost to the point of overwhelming, but I got used to the groove of being around that many people and set my pace working my way around strollers, vendors, city cops and strangers. All were hospitable and nice to me.

I stood in front of Rockefeller
Center in awe of the great tree; the spar-
kle from the lights filled the cold night
air. After barely eating all day out of
nervousness, I came upon a street vendor
that was selling the biggest soft pretzels
I had ever seen. I ate it generously as I
made my way to Times Square where the
lights from the TV screens engulfed me
and sent me spinning with excitement.
From there I made my way back towards
the ferry, skirting side streets and keeping pace as I felt refreshed from all the
excitement of the day. I left the crowds
of people, in the distance, as I made my
way step by step away from the voices,
the sounds and the inescapable noise of
human interaction.

Peaceful and quiet it became,
dark but not ominous, the sounds of
my footsteps the only ones to be heard
a mile away. The harbor appeared and
soon I was back home on the ferry, from
where I started from many hours earli-

er. The cold air was nipping at my face, my smile as wide as could be, staring back at the massive city and waves of people as the ferry shoved forth. I sat down and allowed my heart to rest, content that I had achieved the goal I had set out to do. The present day's events filled my heart and soul, the anticipation I had waited for, for so long, were mellowed and calmed by the sounds of the quiet engine of the ferry. I realized that premonitions do come true if you allow them to become a part of you.

CHAPTER 2

The Baptismal Candle

One by one the priest blessed each of our souls with the sign of the cross drawn onto our foreheads with holy water. I had prepared for this moment for six months, silently hiding who I was on the inside to get the chance to become baptized on the physical plane. I wanted to become baptized and Catholic like Padre Pio, but it was not without hardships. Although I knew Padre Pio was in acceptance of my psychic and mediumship abilities, I knew that others on the physical plane would not be so lenient with bringing a psychic medium into the church to become confirmed. So I hid who I was all throughout the initiation program only going as far as to say that I was a spiritual healer and a follower of Padre Pio's.

I knew in my heart that this was the right thing to do. I was not renouncing who I was by any means; in fact, I was adding on a key component that would help me work more effectively in the future. I was adding an extra layer of protection from God, which is what I needed and although I knew I was a follower of God's grace, I also knew others on the physical plane would be uncomfortable with who I was out of fear and not love. I chose to withhold who I was, so I could obtain my spiritual mastery through the eyes of God on a higher level of existence where only love resides.

A couple of days before my confirmation, I met with a priest, as each one of us in the initiation program was required to do so as part of the rite of passage that was happening before us. He asked me my mission for becoming a Catholic and I told him I have had spiritual experiences with angels and was also a follower of Padre Pio. He exclaimed that he himself had been a supporter of Padre Pio's life and spiritual experiences. The priest welcomed me into his church with open arms, as he did with all of his parishioners. I told him a few more of my spiritual experiences and he told me some more of his own. My talk with the priest ended up being my only confession, I have ever made inside church walls to this day.

The day to become baptized and confirmed into Christ and the church had arrived. This was the day before Easter, as my long-awaited ceremony of anticipation and renewal was here. It was my turn at last to become baptized. I stood up with my ceremonial robe draped over me as I leaned over a fountain filled with holy water. The priest gently took my head and washed away my sins as he poured the cold water over my head and into the fountain. I took my place in line at the front of the church as I took my first communion and was blessed by God. I then took the communion candle. It was lit as I held it between my hands with my head bowed in prayer. It was done. My confirmation name was Pio. I was baptized and confirmed into the church as a Catholic. I hoped Padre Pio would be proud of my decision to follow him in his footsteps.

I exited the church as I breathed a sigh of relief on what I had just accomplished. My soul was happy and safe, but I still had the nagging feeling that something was amiss. I realized that I was sad that I could not tell others in the church who I was or what I practiced. I almost went back in and left a deck of tarot cards in the pew, a calling card of sorts, but alas, I did not.

It took me many years to realize that even though we are all born onto the physical plane with different thoughts, feelings and emotions on various subjects, that it's through these differences that we become one with humanity. Maybe the parishioners couldn't see it, but I could. By keeping silent I achieved my purpose by not only nudging myself further along my spiritual path but by learning to honor the differences between myself and others in a non-judgmental fashion. Expectations and judgements cease to exist with God; it just is.

CHAPTER 3

The Bill in his Pocket

He had been traveling alone for quite some time. A lone wolf he was, on a personal quest of self-discovery. His clothes were ragged, worn and dusty, stained with the dirt of the day. As he spoke to me, I could feel his soul reverberate through his humble and quiet voice. A peaceful soul he was, intrigued with the idea of meeting someone with the same idea of freedom and non-conformity that he had had.

He picked up my book, staying peacefully silent as he flipped through the pages, his silence full of curiosity and attention. After a few moments, his energy started to shift as a spark of hope suddenly shot through his body like lightning . He looked up at me with wonder and held the book in his hands before reaching into his pocket to find a bill in which to pay it with.

My book resonated with him; I could see it in his eyes. He searched every pocket he had one by one, each time coming up empty. By this time, I offered to give him the book for free, not expecting anything in return. He said he wanted to pay me, and I respected him for that.

Finally, in the last pocket he checked, he pulled out a crumpled up old bill, the last one in his possession and handed it to me. I took the crumpled bill and relayed to him how I was glad my book could be of comfort to him. He graciously thanked me and walked back into the crowd from which he came.

He disappeared a few moments later and I sat back in awe that I had just had an eye-opening experience with the mysterious traveler. It made me realize that whoever was meant to read my book would find it, and it made everything I had gone through totally worth it, as my experiences helped another in the process that day.

CHAPTER 4

The Writing on my Palm

Laura examined my hand gently with a magnifying glass. She took care to look at my whole palm in the most inquisitive and direct way. She said that I had the element of fire all over my hand, indicating that I had a lot of strength, desire and determination there. She said that I could not stay in one place for long and that the lines on my palm indicated a need to travel to faraway and exotic places. She also said that my soul was meant to see the world, to feel the crisp sunshine on my face, backpack on my shoulders, and to feel the ground beneath my feet.

Laura mentioned that on my non-dominant hand, which was my left hand, that I came from a past where I used my psychic abilities in that lifetime. I had the lines of an "X" on my left hand, which signified psychic ability was present there. X marks the spot. My right hand, which was my dominant hand, was bringing forth my psychic ability into this lifetime.

What struck me as interesting

was that everything that I was working so hard to achieve in this lifetime was written on my palm. Laura said that the lines reflected my past, present and future and that I was on my path. Just like how my path was written in the stars through astrology, it was also written on my palm in a profound way.

I learned that the lines of one's palm are always changing, and that fate can be directed or redirected depending on our desires and attitudes throughout our lifetime and that our destiny is not so much written in stone but in our hearts, our minds and our soul.

The reality of the situation hit me like a brick. I came from a background of deep knowing and was imparting it onto others in this lifetime. I left that reading with peace in my heart and love in my soul.

CHAPTER 5

Joan of Arc

They whisper to us in the shadows, quietly at first, ignoring hesitation and skepticism from us. Maybe it's to comfort us; maybe it's to let us know that more exists to this life than we realize, or maybe it's to get our attention. Maybe it's for a purpose...

The path was silent, beautiful and absent of people. The sounds of footsteps were only my own, trudging along against the line of trees. I walked past the fallen leaves from past September, the crickets humming softly near my ear as my hands swept past the array of flowers and bushes that surrounded me. They circled above my head, covering the path as they pushed into a narrow opening, similar to that of a deep dark forest. Hints of sunlight burst forth through the trees above and bathed my head in a golden wonder.

I was safe and at peace as I walked on the trail that day. The trail led out to the beach and back again as I sat at the edge of the water, no boats in sight, just the cool summer breeze upon me. The energy of the lake was powerful and it took me a second to get my bearings as I headed back into town to gather my things before I headed home for the day.

I entered a museum that had photographs dating back to the 1800s, involving the history of spirit photography. I left the museum and circled back towards my car to get a quick glimpse and to pay my respects to the local pet cemetery which also dated back to the 1800s. The beautiful and unique gravestones were on the edge of a beautiful forest, surrounded by the blooming trees of summer. It was quiet and serene but humming with the unseen energy of spirits that visited from time to time. Violets and honey suckle, adorned their graves, a tranquil resting place for such majestic animals.

I headed to the local "fairy trail" where energy workers had filled the trail with Reiki. Ornaments of fairies followed each step I took as I ventured further into the forest. I turned back refreshed and renewed, from the Reiki energy that flowed through and around me.

I stopped at the local tree stump where psychic readings had been given for hundreds of years. The pews in front of the stump were empty as I imagined myself in front of an audience someday giving messages to others. I ran into the local bookstore before I headed back to my car. I was looking at one of the items they had for sale when a woman approached me and stared me in the eyes and said that my energy felt similar to that of Joan of Arc.

I was almost embarrassed when she said that and quite skeptical of her comment, when another woman stepped forward and said that she loved reading the history of Joan of Arc. I asked her what her name was and she said "Joan." They came in separately and neither knew the other. Quietly, I thought to myself that maybe Joan of Arc was with me that day, a quiet reminder that they hear us and are listening.

CHAPTER 6

Mysticism & Angels

I held the wand tightly in my right hand
that I had made from copper piping,
quartz crystal points and fulgurite.
Fulgurite was sand that was struck by
lightning. I used it to charge the wand as
I channeled Reiki through it. The name
of my class was called, "healing circle
with the angels." I devised it a month
earlier as I felt a calling to teach it.

   The students gathered around
me as I asked them to hold their hands
in "gassho," which in Reiki culture is
the prayer position. I spoke of the angels
whom I had dealt with in my past, how
the Holy Spirit came to me and how
Archangel Michael was near me as I
spoke. I knelt to take a pause, opened my
channel, took off my energetic cloak and
was officially in my element and glory.

   I clutched my wand tightly as I
extended my arm. Behind each person, I
drew Reiki healing symbols, as well as
the cross and the pentagram for protection. Slowly behind each of their heads, I
recited an angel prayer as I drew ancient

healing symbols down their backs. This was not a Reiki attunement, but a healing ritual that I devised through my own personal channeling.

The tranquil music played in the background as I finished healing the last person. I closed my channel, and had each person open their hands as I placed a little tiny feather inside, a little present from my healing. I drew the sign of the cross on each of their hands and prayed in silence that each one would be healed.

After the ritual ended, I had the class open their eyes as they conveyed the wondrous feelings they had received. Some said they felt their shoulders were lighter, released from stress and worry. One gentleman said with tears in his eyes that he felt something magical and spiritual had happened in that moment, something outside himself that had healed his heart from within.

I was grateful to be my true self that day and to make a difference in someone else's life. Everyone deserves to be healed through the grace and glory of God. All one has to do is ask.

I put my energetic cloak back on and walked out the door, waving goodbye and thanking the owners for having me, my heart fulfilled at being my true self for that moment in time. I was blessed.

CHAPTER 7

The Sunset Colored Aura

I shifted the cards gently in my hands waiting for the next person to arrive. I was surrounded by people and it made me quite nervous as I had never done readings in full view of the public before. In front of me, at the adjacent table was a woman who claimed to talk to angels. To the right of me, people were dipping their toes into electromagnetic water that pulls toxins away from the skin.

The first person sat down, then another and another and before I knew it, I had a whole line of people waiting to be read. My nerves were frayed, as they watched me with anticipation. I respectfully blocked them in an energetic way and focused on my reading at hand. The cards created a story and through them, my intuition began to flow. The gentleman in front of me widened his eyes in surprise, shaking my hand afterwards, feeling more in control of what his future had to hold.

I took a break and circled the fair,

introducing myself to others and eyeing what was for sale. I came to a table with a sign labeled "aura photography" on the front. I took my chances and sat down, excited to see what my aura had to say about my life and well-being. As I began to relax, the aura photographer asked me to think of a happy memory or something that made me feel excited about life in general.

I focused on a happy thought of success and held in my mind's eye the image of prosperity and abundance. When I viewed my printed photograph, I was astonished that my entire aura was bright orange with some red mixed into the picture. Orange was representative of abundance and success. It also had to do with intense creativity as I realized that my energy and vibration were a perfect match for bringing out my endeavors. I was in perfect alignment for manifesting my goals and exactly where I needed to be.

I walked out of the psychic fair

more confident than I had been in ages, realizing that reading for others amongst a crowd was just another lesson my spirit guides wanted me to build upon as I gained strength of will within myself and the world around me. What left with me that day was a sense of confidence and healthy ego.

CHAPTER 8

A Rude Awakening

I sat down as the card reader proceeded to lay five cards out onto the table for my tarot reading. She didn't interpret them but stayed silent. After a few minutes, I asked what she thought each of the cards meant and she said that the descriptions were on the bottoms of each of the cards and that I could read them myself. She didn't know me or know I was a tarot reader. There was no reading, but she charged me $45.00 to interpret my own cards.

The next reader was even worse. She was rude, didn't make any sense and I left realizing that this is what the public dealt with sometimes. There are more fake psychics, mediums and tarot readers out there than honest ones and the psychological damage that is inflicted onto society because of this was horrifying.

It made me realize why I went to a psychic fair, seemingly in the middle of nowhere, that day. I felt my spirit guides wanted me to realize how important my work was in helping others and even though I already knew this, I don't think I realized the deception coming from others until I witnessed it with my own two eyes. It made my work that much more important and justified.

CHAPTER 9

Lady Magdalene

She gazed up at me with her crystal blue eyes. A crystal child she was, born to my sister, a psychic woman herself with a heart of gold. I gripped Magdalene's tiny hand in mine, promising to be her guardian angel and reveling in the fact that I saw in her what I saw in me, infinite potential to be a beacon of light to help those in a sea of darkness.

My hand grasped her beautiful blonde hair, brushing it gently away from her eyes, awaiting the day when I could tell her the hidden knowledge, I had kept secret for so many years. The universal knowledge passed down to me from the other side, from multiple generations passed, a seemingly echo of a former life.

I felt angels around her as I held her in my arms once more and I knew she would be protected from here on out. With my help, I would teach her the secrets of the unknown. I put my tarot cards in her little hands, and let her feel and touch them as she marveled at the colors and details. I patiently explained each one, even if she was too tiny to understand them.

She was a fast learner and as soon as she learned to talk, she would pull tarot cards for my sister and me. She could not yet read, but gazed at them in wonder, handing them to me to explain each card to her, as her ancestors before her did in previous lifetimes. My sister then brought out her pendulum and placed it over Magdalene's head. The end of the pendulum flew around her head in wide circular motions, so big for someone so small.

I checked her astrology chart and psychic, she was. She had five planets in the 12th house alone, the house of psychic ability and the unconscious mind. How this would play out I did not know, but after my sister and I put her down for a nap, the live stream baby video showed orbs all around her.

The beginning of her spiritual

journey had already started at such a young age. The next-day Magdalene and I sat at our birthday party together as her birthday was only a day-after mine on August 27th. Soul twins we were and I would protect her indefinitely. I sat down beside her calling her my "Little Lady," just as my grandmother did when I was young as she proceeded to blow out the candles, her wishes revealed in time.

CHAPTER 10

Let their paws show you the way

I have had many experiences receiving signs from animals. This has helped me to conclude that our souls are intertwined with theirs and that the connection and bond do not cease when our pets cross over. They go to Heaven just like we do, and they do indeed have a soul as well.

Duncan, the terrier mix, of one of my family members, crossed over from an unexpected illness. I meditated on his energy one evening and received the message that there was a woman there to greet him as he crossed over to the other side. She was a slim woman dressed in a suit jacket and skirt with her hair pulled back in a tight bun. She was managerial in nature but oh so kind and gentle.

Duncan was happy with his tail wagging behind him. A happy puppy he was and continued to be through his transition. He held his head high in a playful manner as the woman escorted him over. He was genuinely excited for his new beginning and not scared in the least, as you see crossing over is more natural for animals, as they follow their own intuition and guidance with ease. They understand energy, spirits and Heaven and transition for them is as natural as breathing.

Duncan was safe as he crossed to the other side with his heavenly escort. We are all greeted by someone on the other side when we cross over, even if we don't have any family members on the physical plane who we recognize or are close to.

Animals can also be guides after they have crossed over. Our one cat named "Hobo" escaped through a basement window and was lost for days. We put food out for him, but he would not come home. One night after he had been out for several days, I had a very vivid dream about our other cat "Boo-Boo," who had departed from this Earth many years ago. Through "feelings of thoughts" he told me that "Hobo" would be arriving home and that "Boo-Boo" was guiding him.

The next morning, "Hobo" showed up at the back door meowing in anticipation to be let back in. "Hobo" was safe just like "Boo-Boo" had promised me. If it had not been for "Boo-Boo's' guidance, 'Hobo," might have never made it home that day.

Your pets have signs for you. They might not communicate through words, but they will always communicate through their heart and soul. Pay attention and listen to what they are trying to tell you, as they will be there when you venture home to Heaven.

CHAPTER 11

The Skies Eyes

Sometimes when you stare up at the moon on a crisp black night, she beckons and calls to you, her pull towards you undeniable, for she is a psychic moon. She is reincarnated as the high priestess on the physical plane, the owner and keeper of secret knowledge, knowledge that is waiting to be revealed if you ask the right questions. If you do, you will own a key to her soul.

We are energy; the universe is energy. The planets, stars and moon are energy. That energy pulls on our heart strings and helps us to understand patterns in our lives and within ourselves.

When we are born, an energetic signature is created and can be read through an astrology chart. The chart includes different sections called "houses" that include one's sun sign, moon sign and rising sign.

Astrology may influence our personalities to an extent, but I do not feel that it dictates our future. Our future is held in the decisions we make, our thoughts and emotions, like rays of light, shooting out into the universe and coming back to us like a boomerang, a rhythmic dance of energy.

Our true purpose lies in helping others through the creator, our past lives sitting on the sidelines just waiting to be revealed. Our purpose is in the mind of the beholder, literally. Follow the star to your destination; gaze up at the vastness of the universe during a crystal clear, deep dark, black night. Breathe in the fresh air, the cool undertones of the air against your skin; breathe in the richness and the glorious wonder of God's creation. Be yourself. Be you. Be free.

CHAPTER 12

Forgiveness holds many colors

Ten years after my spiritual awakening commenced, the confusion on why this happened to me in the first place left me and turned into acceptance. I emerged full of hope and viewed my life on the physical plane from an outside perspective. Instead of being consumed by my awakening, I was in control of it.

The thorns removed themselves one by one, slowly and gently as if wind took hold and replaced them with something else, something unknown to me for so many years; a quickening of my soul became apparent as my heart began to thud in my ears. The thorns gently uncoiled from my arms, down my body and away from my feet, I was free of the chaos that obsessed my days and nights for so long.

My life force energy was flowing again, out of my hands and through my feet, curving around my waist and outwards towards the universe to receive the gifts from Heaven. I was no longer bound by the chains of my own doing. I allowed myself to hold forgiveness for others as I moved towards my future. Instead of holding my breath, I took in everything and allowed myself the wonder of new experiences. I could breathe for the first time in years.

I was witnessing my light emerge into something more, a communion between the physical plane and God. I emerged like a cicada and allowed myself to feel the depths of my own being, not afraid but full of hope that one can progress and grow into something else entirely. I was free…

CHAPTER 13

Spiritual Mastery

My climb up the mountain to reach my higher self was not for the faint of heart. It was full of burden, regret, heartache and loss but was also filled with illumination, enrichment and endowment of spiritual gifts.

The road to self-mastery, for me, was a lonely one. It was quiet on top of the mountain as the winds echoed through the caverns of my past. The farther I moved away from the chaos, the more aware I became of myself and God.

The path of the pilgrim is to become self-aware, not just aware of one's self and soul, but to become aware of eternity and life after death. You must learn to see the divine through the eyes of those who have crossed over. You must see what they see, feel what they feel and touch what they touch. You must grab their extended hand and push yourself upwards towards a higher level of existence. You must awaken and see the light, for these spirits are still alive…

ABOUT THE AUTHOR

Amber is a Usui/Tibetan Reiki Master Teacher & Practitioner and a Registered Karuna Reiki® Master Teacher & Practitioner and is a graduate of 'The Anastasi System of Psychic Development.' She holds two degrees, one in art and design from Millersville University of Pennsylvania and the other in photography from Harrisburg Area Community College.

She has been featured on numerous radio shows spreading awareness to others through her story and work. She has taught Reiki to students from all over the world spreading her light to others for the world to see. Amber is a traveler always seeking the next adventure with her home base in Pennsylvania.

ambernightingale.net